←: TRUE TALES of RESCUE :→

Sweet Senior Pups

KAMA EINHORN
PHOTOGRAPHS BY **VIRGIL OCAMPO**

HOUGHTON MIFFLIN HARCOURT

Boston   New York

hmhco.com

The text type was set in Jolly Good Sans.

Library of Congress Cataloging-in-Publication Data
Names: Einhorn, Kama, 1969-author.Title: Sweet senior pups / Kama Einhorn ;
photographs by TK. Description: Boston : Houghton Mifflin Harcourt, [2018] |
Series: True Tales of Rescue | Audience: Age 7-10. | Audience: Grade 4 to 6. | Includes
bibliographical references and index. Identifiers: LCCN 2017044043 | ISBN 9781328767035
Subjects: LCSH: Dogs—Aging—Juvenile literature
.Classification: LCC SF426.5 .E37 2018 | DDC 636.7--dc23LC
record available at https://lccn.loc.gov/2017044043

Manufactured in China
SCP 10 9 8 7 6 5 4 3 2 1
4500725266

This book is based on the true stories of rescued dogs, and it's full of real facts about senior pups.
But it's also "creative" nonfiction—because dogs don't talk, at least not in ways that humans can
understand! Some dogs in this story are combinations of several different ones, and certain details,
including locations, events, and timing have been changed, and some human dialogue has been
reconstructed from memory.

This book is not a manual on senior dog rescue, or meant to provide
any actual advice or directions on caring for any animal.

For Val, Margee, and Greg Lynch

CONTENTS

PART 1: RESCUE

PART 2: RECOVERY

PART 3: REHABILITATION

HOPE & HAVEN: ANIMAL SANCTUARIES

A sanctuary is a safe space, usually created by kind humans, in which living beings are kept safe from harm.

Animal sanctuaries are protected places for injured, orphaned, or threatened animals—usually wildlife, but also cats and dogs. At the Senior Dog Sanctuary of Maryland (SDSM), homeless dogs over age six are loved and cared for until the people there can find them another home. If they don't, the dogs stay there for the rest of their lives, getting lots of hugs and belly rubs.

The dog in the Sanctuary's logo has low hips, because many senior dogs, especially larger breeds, have problems with their hip joints. A sunrise tells you that a day is beginning, and a sunset tells you it's ending. So Val Lynch, the sanctuary founder, made sure that the sign looked like both, for even at the end of their lives, dogs can still get the new

At sanctuaries, humans lend a helping hand.

beginnings they need. They can have new chapters in their stories, chapters in which they feel the safety and love that they once had and lost, or that they may never have known.

People who run sanctuaries are serious about their work, but they wish they didn't have to do it in the first place. They all hope for a day when they're not needed—a day when the world is a better place for animals.

There's plenty of heartbreak involved in any sanctuary's story, but there's also good news. People who help animals are everywhere. And the more you know about why sanctuaries are important and what you can do to help, the better off all living creatures will be.

SANCTUARY STEPS

Each sanctuary is different, but they all do some or all of the following things in the order below. The Senior Dog Sanctuary of Maryland handles all four of these phases:

- **Rescue:** Humans remove animals from danger and bring them to safety.

- **Recovery:** Veterinarians and trained staff treat the animals for injuries or illness, decide on a recovery plan, and help them rest and heal.

- **Rehabilitation:** Animals who were scared, injured, or homeless when they were rescued begin to trust their human caregivers and start feeling safer, healthier, and more loved. They start having fun, just like normal dogs.

- **Release:** The staff and volunteers help the dogs find "forever homes," or, if they're so sick that they won't get any better, they make sure they have peaceful, painless deaths.

THREE BLIND MICE

TO: The next dog (or dogs) who will stay in this room

FROM: Mino, Jack, and Buffy, the current residents

Welcome to the Senior Dog Sanctuary of Maryland, and to
your little room. I'm Mino, and these are my roommates,
Jack and Buffy. Some dogs here have their own rooms,
but lots of us double or triple up, especially if we came
here together or if we're small, blind, or deaf (or any
combination of these things). We like to smell and feel
other dogs near us. We're pack animals, after all! The
three of us are like the Three Musketeers.

You may be wondering why it's just me writing this
letter from all three of us. It's because I have the
loudest voice. I'm a real barker, so I'm going to blab
our secret: This is a lucky room! The three of us
became best pals, and then, all on the same weekend,
different people decided to adopt us! Each of us will go
to our new homes soon.

We were in bad shape when we were first rescued and
brought here, and you probably are, too. But things

changed fast. The staff and the volunteers helped us get healthier and happier, and of course they found us our new homes. But while you wait, you'll have a great time. We could be happy here forever, but there are more dogs who need help, and there's space for only twenty-six of us. So if we leave, more dogs get rescued. But some dogs do stay here for the rest of their lives, and it's a good time!

Lots of our adoptions happen because the humans post our photos online so that people fall in love with us (not too hard to do). Many of us have become social media stars! This place is full of stories, and lots of those stories make it onto people's computer screens all over the world. Our online photos are like little commercials. Some humans say, "bad things happen in threes," but I think it's the opposite: Good things happen in threes.

Mino

The people here call us the Three Blind Mice because we're all tiny and blind (or part blind). But all three of us get by in our own doggy ways.

We use our hearts, and our hearts work perfectly!

We'll tell you everything you need to know about this place. Enjoy your lucky room!

Oh, and in case you didn't know, we senior dogs are nicknamed "sugarfaces" because of our white muzzles. Maybe our faces turn white on the outside because we're so sweet on the inside. In any case, lots of us look like we've stuck our faces in a bag of sugar.

 ## Senior Dog Sanctuary of Maryland

Heeeere's Mino! He's a fifteen-year-old, fourteen-pound golden Pomeranian. Mr. Mino loves feeling the sun on his face and is always poking his nose high into the air, like he's trying to sniff (or kiss!) the sunshine. Mino is blind, but he's learned his way around just fine. He uses his sense of hearing most of all, and we think he overhears just about everything around here! Mino uses his sense of touch very well too, and once he feels your hands on him, he softens his whole body into your arms.

For Mino, it's all about the love. #olddogslovedeep #stillreadytolove

250 Likes   100 Loves

👍 **Like**   ❤ **Love**   💬 **Comment**

 Tom C.: What a little ball of light. Good luck, Mino! 🖤 🖤 🖤

 Opal R.: He looks like a little lion! I wish I could take him. 🦁

 Cara L.: I'm really rooting for you, young man. 🐾 🐾

 Senior Dog Sanctuary of Maryland

Meet our latest arrival—spunky, sassy, social-butterfly Buffy! She's a twelve-year-old miniature pinscher (Min Pin) who's fired up brightly by her own unique spark. Buffy weighs seven pounds, but her personality seems to contradict that low number—her energy is so oversized, she wants to be everywhere at once. Her best trick is twirling like a ballerina!

Buffy is blind in one eye and she's had cancer, but since her skin tumors were removed, she's been doing very well for longer than anyone had predicted. Her tongue hangs from the side of her mouth because she doesn't have teeth to hold it in anymore . . . and she looks pretty darn cute! Buffy practically explodes with spirit, reminding you that it's not the years in your life, it's the life in your years.

204 Likes   76 Loves

👍 **Like**   ❤️ **Love**   💬 **Comment**

 Terry D.: What a tiny thing. You can see her big spirit. Good luck, Buffy! 🐕 🖤

 Colleen G.: I love Buffy. I hope she gets adopted soon. 🦴🦴🦴

 Cassidy G.: Buffy is a spunky, sweet girl! 😍

 ## Senior Dog Sanctuary of Maryland

Sweet, sleepy Jack is a fourteen-year-old French poodle, but you might think you are looking at a gentle gray lamb with a little hunchback! Jack's favorite thing is to be swaddled in a blanket and held and rocked like a baby. He's blind and deaf, but that doesn't stop him from giving and receiving all the love he can while enjoying some treats and fresh air every day. Even though he can't see or hear, when it comes to the important things in life, Jack knows more than a lot of us.

For Jack, it's all about the comfy-cozy.

256 Likes   123 Loves

👍 Like   ❤ Love   💬 Comment

 Marge G.: Jack's a great guy. Come meet him!

 John P.: I wish I could adopt him!

 Pam B.: Good luck, old fella!

Sanctuary Sugarface Stars

It takes a long time for a soul to get this sweet! Cub prefers that his muzzle be called silver, not white.

Bruce looks like he got into the powdered doughnuts in the people's coffee room.

Frost is a sweet honey-boy with a muzzle to prove it. He's a real golden oldie!

Marley the salt-and-pepper fella: His face may be white, but his heart is pure gold. There is no shame in growing old.

Buffy demonstrates the
"sugarface" concept.

Oh, before I forget, here's your schedule. Each dog's
day is a little different, but here's the basic idea.

A Day at SDSM

Dawn: Doze.

Sunrise: Early-morning cuddles, petting, or scratching (your choice) with volunteers. Walk #1. Breakfast. Outdoor playtime #1. Morning medications.

Daytime: Lunch and walk #2! Outdoor playtime #2.

Afternoon: Walk #3.

Dusk: Outdoor playtime #3.

Sunset: Walk #4. Dinner. (This is when the barking gets really loud!) Evening medications.

Twilight: Walk #5! (How lucky are we?)

Night: Time for a long snooze.

Once in a while:

- House calls or visits to vet
- Beauty hour/Spa time (when the groomer visits)
- Book buddies (when kids come read to us!)
- A visit to the dog house downstairs (It's a real apartment, where we can get comfy on couches and sit around with the people.)

Here's what the people here say about adopting a sugarface!

 Senior Dog Sanctuary of Maryland

Five Reasons to Adopt a Senior Dog
from Sassy, one of SDSM's old ladies:

1. We know everything already! When you get a young dog, you spend lots of time training and teaching. Our personalities are already well set, so it's likely that what you see is what you get!

2. We're usually pretty mellow and don't need as much activity. We'd prefer to curl up with you as you read, watch television, or sit in front of the fire. And we won't wake you up early in the morning!

3. We're already past our "chewing and destroying the house" phase.

4. We're not as "needy" as younger pups. We love your hugs and kisses, but we usually won't drive you crazy begging for them!

5. We depend on you and are so grateful to you. We'll be your best friends for the rest of our lives.

PART 1

ReSCUE

Getting SAFE

CHAPTER 1

OLD DOGS, NEW LIVES

We're just like you, buddy. We didn't have homes until the sanctuary rescued us. We were having some of the worst days of our lives.

We each have a story. Some of us were living on the street, cold, sick, and wet, eating whatever we could find. Some of us once had people who loved us, but they died or went into nursing homes and couldn't find anyone to take us in. Sometimes we got left behind when our people moved away. Lots of us were brought to shelters that didn't have enough room for us, and old dogs in shelters usually take a long time to get adopted, if that happens at all.

The road to my 🐾
Heart 🐾
🐾 is paved
🐾 with paw prints

Every dog gets his or her pawprint on the wall upon arrival.
The pawprint path winds all around the lobby!

But things got better for all of us one day
when we saw a kind face, heard a soft
voice, and felt a gentle hand on our fur
(the people here hug us and love us up
no matter how dirty, smelly, or matted we
are!). For some of us, that face, voice, and
touch was Val's. For others, it was his son
Greg's or one of the many staff members

or volunteers here. They sometimes drive for hours to pick us up from another shelter or home!

Here at Senior Dog Sanctuary we get our own space, with our own toys and blankets. Those of us who share a room figure out whose spot is whose. Jack's spot is inside a mini-doghouse made of soft, sturdy cloth. It's a little hut, and sometimes he gets stuck in it! I like the hut, too, and Jack's pretty good at sharing it.

We get warm baths—for some of us, our first. I'm a big fan of bubbles and suds.

Colleen and Cassidy are two of my favorite volunteers.

Jessica, a volunteer, loves to kiss me.

If we're sick, we get the medicine we need. The volunteers walk us at least five times a day and let us sniff around all we want. We run in the huge play yard, make friends, and enjoy the sun. We get to know the other dogs' smells. Most of all, we learn that there are people we can count on. Being rescued means we can finally relax.

23

CHAPTER 2

BORN TO RESCUE

Val's been rescuing dogs since 1949, when he was just eight years old! That was before people talked about things like adopting a pet or animal rescue. World War II had just ended, and his family (along with many others) was poor. Having a pet was an extra expense people couldn't afford, and many heartbroken families brought their pets to the dog pound, which is sort of like a shelter. A dogcatcher went around the neighborhood and brought stray dogs there, too, and most of them never found homes. I've heard Val tell visitors the whole story.

Val has always loved animals. As a kid, he'd go to the Bronx Zoo and stare at the creatures, trying to read their minds. He

Val Lynch at age 5 and age 12

rescued his very first dog, a ten-pound
black-and-white mutt, on a rainy summer
afternoon. He'd been playing stickball with
his friends, and on his way home he saw the
pup, soaking wet and trembling, in an alley
near the local bakery. The little dog was all
hunched up against the wet brick wall, head
down, like he was trying to make himself
invisible.

Val knelt down and reached out his hand (now he knows better, and he warns people that's not safe!), but the dog backed away and cowered. So Val just sat down and kept his hand out. The dog seemed curious, and Val moved a little closer. This continued until the dog began licking his hand, and soon Val took off his T-shirt and picked the dog up, wrapping him in his shirt. The dirty, shivering dog buried his head in Val's armpit. He seemed to know that Val was a good human. Val carried the drippy bundle home.

Val talked to him, repeating the same three words: "You're okay, baby." Then he started repeating another three-word phrase: "You're safe now." And before he even reached his apartment, he'd named the dog Shaky (he's used the same name on a few other shaky dogs since then!). But the second his mom saw Shaky, she said the

three words Val had been hoping not to hear:
"He can't stay."

Val's heart had been full of hope. Now his
heart sank, but his voice stayed steady. "It's
okay. I'll take care of him in my room until I
figure it out. It'll just be a few days."

Val took Shaky, still shaking hard, to his
room, where he covered him in some towels
and hugged him until he was shivering only
a little. Val was thinking of a plan the whole
time. He knew that stores paid newspapers
to print their ads, but he didn't have any
money to print an ad for Shaky. This was
before copy machines, and Val and his mom
didn't have a telephone. So he asked his
mom for five index cards and then got Shaky
settled under his small wooden desk with a
bowl of leftovers he'd cut up. Then he sat at
his desk and began creating his very first

adoption listings—a stack of index card ads
that looked like this:

CAN YOU HELP?

This is Shaky. He's a good dog.

I found him on Briggs Avenue on Tuesday in
the alley near the bakery.

He's very sweet and he seems healthy. He'll
make a really good friend.

If you think you could give him a nice home,
please meet us at the corner of Grand Concourse and
Kingsbridge Road at 4:00 tomorrow.

I will introduce you, and you can decide if you want to keep him.

On each card, Val used the "5 W's and an H" trick that his
third-grade teacher had taught him for writing reports—
make sure to say who, what, when, where, why, and how.

That night, Val let Shaky sleep on a towel on
his bed with him. In the morning, he handed
the cards out to two neighborhood boys who
he thought might have nice parents with a
little extra money for dog food. Then he went

to his small neighborhood grocery store and handed the owner a card. The grocer smiled, and said he was sorry, but he couldn't have a dog. So Val asked the grocer if he could put the card in the store window, and the grocer said yes. Back in his apartment building, Val slipped the remaining cards under some neighbors' doors.

He didn't know if anyone would come to the corner the next day at 4:00, but when his mom was out, he gave Shaky a warm bubble bath just in case. Shaky loved it. Val brought him to the corner and waited. No one came. "Don't worry, Shaky," Val said, even though he was pretty worried himself. "It's just the first day. I'll keep trying."

The next day, someone came to meet Val and Shaky, but then decided he couldn't afford to keep a dog. Val went home and

made more ads. Weeks passed; very few
people came to the corner. When they
did come, they had different reasons for
saying no. But Val started to notice that
some of his ads got more people to come
than others did, so he kept changing
them, figuring out which ones worked
best. He looked at ads in the newspaper
and paid attention to how they were
written.

Val's mother was getting impatient. Val
kept telling people about Shaky. He talked
to anyone who would listen—his teachers,
the baker, the police officers he saw in the
neighborhood, and the butcher, who started
saving scraps of meat for Shaky every day.

Four months went by. Then, one afternoon,
someone came to the corner and said she'd
love to adopt Shaky.

And just like that, Shaky had a real home.

Val was hooked on dog rescue. With each dog he found, he got faster and better at finding him or her a home. He figured out how to tell if a dog was blind or deaf. He created a filing system for his notes and records for each dog. He asked his friends to help him, and they did. He found larger, sturdier pieces of paper and started making better ads for the butcher's window; and the butcher kept giving Val meat scraps.

Val saved around seventy dogs before he went into the United States Air Force at age twenty-one. Soon he got married, and when he got an air force job in Illinois for a few years, he and his wife moved into their own home. Now they could adopt dogs of their own.

Sometimes when Val's talking to us, he calls himself "Grampi."

So the Senior Dog Sanctuary of Maryland really started in 1949, although no one realized it until now . . . seventy years later!

Maybe Val understands us blind dogs so well because he has only one eye himself. That happened when he got hurt in the air force. But I don't need to see Val's face. I feel his heart. And I recognize his voice and his hands. He's a good belly-rubber, and he doesn't mind sloppy dog kisses all over his face!

And that's how Val became a rescuer. Now we'll tell you how he and his team rescued us.

CHAPTER 3

SUNRISE STORIES

Some people say that "the darkest hour is right before the dawn." That means just when a situation seems the worst, that's when it's about to get a little better. After every long, dark night, the sky gets lighter, the sun comes up, and soon it's shining down all over your fur. The darkness feels like forever ago. That's how we hope most rescue stories will end.

I, Mino, have a pretty simple rescue story. I lived in a real home since I was a puppy. Then one day my people just drove me here, left me with Val, and drove away. I never figured out why they didn't want me anymore. I'm a very good dog.

Val picked me up right away, and I sniffed his face. He told my people that I was welcome

When I arrived, I had two big problems—both of my eyeballs!

here and that I would be well cared for. I was so grumpy, though—my eyes had been infected for a while, and they were always hurting. It had really gotten me down. But Val kissed my muzzle, and said, "You're okay, baby."

Like all the dogs here, I spent my first nights alone in a special quarantine room until the people knew I was healthy enough to be with other dogs. It was a bad time for me. Val put on some nice music to help me feel less lonely all night, but I was really sad.

Soon, though, a volunteer plopped me right into my new room, where Jack and another small dog, Terrence, were both asleep. I missed my people, and I was still confused, but I lay down in my new little bed. I felt Jack

At 17, Terrence was the oldest dog here. He stood crooked because he'd been hit by a car.

come over, sniff me, and snuggle his warm, fuzzy body right up against mine. Just like that, I knew I was going to be okay. The people kept checking that the three of us were getting along; we absolutely were.

Speaking of Jack, he's snoozing, as usual. So I'll tell you what I know about his rescue.

A hunter found him as a stray dog. That means he was wandering alone and didn't appear to have a home. He was wet and matted when the hunter spotted him in a field on a country road in southwest Virginia, a poor little sugar lamb! His fur was so overgrown, the hunter could barely tell he was a dog.

It seemed certain that someone had left him out there—it was too far from any homes or buildings for him to have walked there by

himself. For lots of us homeless dogs, the people who rescue us will never know what happened before they came along. And Jack has never told me—maybe he just doesn't remember. He's been a little forgetful lately.

The hunter called the local humane society to come get him, and the vet there guessed that he was about fourteen or fifteen years old. She removed the few bad teeth he had left, and he was such a sorry sight that Cindy, one of the shelter directors at that humane society, decided to foster him so he could recover in a home instead of at the shelter. Cindy named him Jacques, after the French ocean explorer Jacques Cousteau. She and her husband are divers, and she kept thinking of their experiences diving at night in the dark water, feeling both blind and deaf. Plus, Jack is a French poodle!

Jack's fur was so long and matted that it hurt—it was pulling on his skin. First the shelter workers shaved Jack. His skin still looked pretty bad underneath, so they used oatmeal shampoo to treat it.

It took months for all his fur to grow back, but here's handsome, fancy Jack after his first grooming here.

Cindy fostered Jack for seven weeks, then brought him here. Cindy was in foster care herself when she was a baby, and then she was adopted; she felt that she could really understand dogs in his situation.

They put Jack in the room with Terrence and me, and we both sniffed him and agreed that he seemed like a fine fellow.

Jack got his own little coat. Like many seniors, his body couldn't keep itself warm enough.

Soon the dog groomer, a very kind and
gentle guy, decided to take Terrence
home with him. Jack and I were happy for
Terrence, but sad for ourselves. We missed
our old lopsided friend. I secretly hoped
Jack wouldn't be taken away, too. I felt a
little selfish hoping for such a thing, but
I just didn't want to be alone or live with
anyone else—Jack was a perfect roommate.
But no one took him away, and a few months
later we met tiny, shiny Buffy in the "little
dog" outdoor play group and then she
moved into our room. She's certainly been
"living large" here. She's standing up and
prancing around on her hind legs for treats.
I guess the treat right now is that she gets
to tell her story.

I'm sure Buffy won't explain certain details
of how she was found, because she lives
in the moment, moving (leaping, actually)

forward and never looking back. And right now I'd say her moment is pretty fabulous, judging from the ballerina moves I have to put up with all the time. It almost seems like she's forgotten about her past (which would be nice, of course).

Anyway, Buffy was found in a dog crate in an alley behind a building. No one knew who left her there or why. The animal shelter people picked her up after someone called them.

I, Mino, understand a lot of things, as you can tell. But as long as I live, I'll never understand how a person could just leave Buffy or Jack out there alone. *Big sigh.*

Once we arrive here, it's clear that these people are different. They have a whole system set up just to take care of us. First,

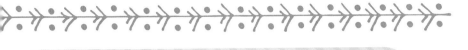

MY SUNRiSE STORY

by Buffy

I'm a southwest Virginia girl, just like Jack! Except Jack's a boy, LOL. The Humane Society of Pulaski County, Virginia, rescued both of us. I still look young, but the people can guess our age by looking at our teeth, and when they saw what an "old lady" I was, they knew I'd have a better chance of getting adopted if I was here. They called Val to see if there was room . . . and it was my lucky day!

The only real problem was that I had loose teeth and infected gums, so my mouth felt like it was on fire. Once the vet removed all my teeth, I felt like a million bucks. For the first time in a long time, I started to feel like a young princess. And I got treated like one, too. The people taught me how to dance like a ballerina, and I've been prancing around for treats ever since!

Mino and Jack and I became BFFs, and soon I got put in their room with them. Hip hip hooray for me, hip hip hooray for us! Getting used to life here was as easy as one-two-three.

we get a collar with a sanctuary tag on it, with the phone number, in case we ever get lost somehow. This stays on even when we go to our forever homes—because we're always welcome back here for any reason. Once a sanctuary dog, always a sanctuary dog!

They put our names on a folder and put all our vet records and notes and forms inside. We each get a little plastic bin with our names and photos on the outside. Inside the bin are all our medicines, special toys, and our old tags and collars if we came with any. Our names get added to big whiteboards on the wall so people can keep track of our walks, feedings, medications, and daily notes.

Once a week the groomers come and give eight lucky dogs a bubble bath and a haircut, all for free. They even use a nice, warm blow-dryer. When they're finished,

*Virgil the photographer and his team
volunteer to take fancy pictures of the dogs.*

many of us look the prettiest we've ever
looked in our lives. We get out pictures
taken, and the people put them online to tell
the world about us.

Sometimes we notice that the sanctuary
people are feeling sad and frustrated. It
might be when there's no extra room here
and they have to say no to helping another

dog. It might be because a dog arrives so sick that they can't save him. And it might be because they're thinking about how many dogs out there never get rescued in the first place. That's when they read this sign on the wall.

You can't change the
world by saving one dog,
but for that one dog,
the world is
forever changed.

And over and over, the people here remind one another of this story about a boy and some starfish.

The Starfish Story

A man walked along a beach. There had just been a big storm, but it was sunny again, and the man saw that hundreds, maybe even thousands, of starfish had washed up onto the sand. They were drying in the hot sun, and they would not live long out of water.

The man noticed a boy standing near the waves in the distance, and as he walked closer, the saw the boy picking things up from the sand and throwing them into the water. As he got even closer, he saw that those things were starfish. The man sighed. The boy would never be able to save all those starfish.

"Young man," he called. "I admire what you're trying to do, but I'm afraid your efforts won't amount to much. There are hundreds, maybe thousands of starfish here. You'll never get to all of them before they dry up in the sun and die."

The boy bent down, picked up another starfish, and threw It hard into the waves. Then he turned around and smiled proudly at the man.

"I know it," he said. "But I sure made a difference for that one!"

Getting rescued is the beginning of a new day for us—a good and bright day. And I do love the sunshine.

People bring and send us all kinds of stuff, like food, toys, and doggie coats and sweaters. But the donations we get the most of are blankets! I think everyone just wants to get us warm and cozy.

We love our cozy blankets, but when we're wiggly, bedtime can turn into a slumber PARTY!

PART 2

RECOVERY

Getting BETTER

CHAPTER 4
VETS TO
THE RESCUE

First things first. Once we're rescued, the people's top priority is to get us as healthy as they can.

That has its challenges with us old dogs. We have lots of the same health problems as older people do, and we have similar needs. We need foods that are easy to chew and digest, and we need more time indoors because we don't move as well as we once did. We have to go to the doctor more. We might become forgetful, and we might need extra help getting around.

Of course, we don't live as long as people. I'm fifteen, which for a little dog equals about

seventy-six "human years." (I'm small, and small dogs usually live longer than large dogs. Scientists have some ideas about this, but they're still trying to figure out exactly why!)

HOW DOGS aGE COMPaReD TO HUMaNS			
SIZE OF DOG	SMALL	MEDIUM	LARGE
AGE OF DOG	AGE IN HUMAN YEARS		
1 Year	15	15	15
2	24	24	24
3	28	28	28
4	32	32	32
5	36	36	36
6	40	42	45
7	44	47	50
8	48	51	55
9	52	56	61
10	56	60	66
11	60	65	72
12	64	69	77
13	68	74	82
14	72	78	88
15	76	83	93
16	80	87	120

The oldest known dog lived to be twenty-nine years old! Who knows? Maybe I'll break the record. I'm full of surprises.

Lots of us old dogs have diabetes, which means we have too much sugar in our blood. The vet explains it this way: We get sugar from all our food (not just sweets!), and it goes into our bloodstream. Then the pancreas (an organ near our stomach) makes a chemical called insulin. Insulin helps the sugar get into our cells so we have energy.

But if we have diabetes, we don't have enough insulin, or it's not working right all the time. The sugar stays in our blood, which means it's not getting into our cells. So we get insulin shots, and we're okay. The disease kinda makes perfect sense for a sugarface. Too much sugar, get it?

Hunter's hips sagged because of arthritis.

Another total bummer of getting older is arthritis, a condition that wears away our joints and gives us major aches and pains. There's medicine for it, and sometimes we even get massages. But it's a real pain in the hips and the knees! The people here know we have it when we start using one leg more than the others, when it seems as if we're having a hard time sitting or standing, when we hesitate to run, jump, or climb stairs—or when we suddenly get grumpier than usual.

Obviously we can't use words to explain to the people how we're feeling, so they watch us closely to try to figure it out. And they really know how to take good care of us.

Senior aches and pains can make Gus very grumpy.

CHAPTER 5

A SPACE AND A PLACE

I'd been diabetic for a long time, and it made me blind. I hadn't been getting the insulin shots or the special diabetic dog food I needed. And I had glaucoma, which means too much pressure inside your eyes. My eyes bulged out. My buggy eyes were constantly infected—that's why they'd been hurting me so much. The vet told the people that I'd feel much better if he removed my eyes, and he was totally right. Together, they figured out a plan to manage my diabetes with insulin shots and the right food. I had my own little place to rest and recuperate from the surgery.

Sarge catches a treat.

A few volunteers make the yummiest treats just for us diabetic dogs. Some dogs get so excited by these treats they turn into "alligator dogs"—they don't know where their mouths end and the treats begin! But I always try to take my treats very gently.

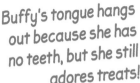

Buffy's tongue hangs out because she has no teeth, but she still adores treats!

MY LONG JOURNEY
by Jack

Hello there. I'm Jack, and my recovery story has a few different chapters. At Cindy's, I was so tired that I slept in an old baby playpen for three whole days! Recuperating at Cindy's house gave me the peace and quiet I needed; she only woke me up to hand-feed me plain boiled chicken and rice or duck with sweet potato. I loved those warm, mashed-up mixtures, and slowly I began gaining weight.

When I finally had more energy, I started moving around outside the playpen. I felt safe and relaxed with Cindy in her home, so I absolutely hated it whenever she left. Once, I barked so hard and for so long that I hurt my throat, and she knew it was time for me to be in a different place—one with people and other dogs around me all the time.

On our last day together, Cindy took me to the beach and helped me put my toes in the water. I had never been there. I lay in the sand and felt the sun and the wind on my skin (my fur hadn't grown back yet). It felt so good.

The drive here was five hours each way, so Cindy organized a "rescue relay," which is something rescue people do. Different volunteers each drive one section of the trip. Cindy and I drove together for an hour, and then we said goodbye. She cried and promised me she'd visit soon. Then she handed me over to the next driver, who also kissed me, and we drove about an hour until the next person met us. And so on until we got here.

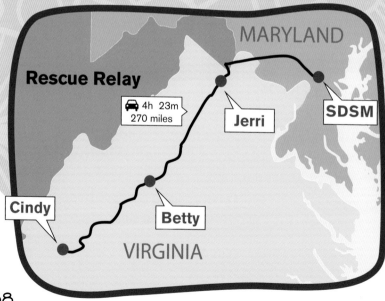

Rescue Relay

🚗 4h 23m
270 miles

MARYLAND

Jerri

SDSM

Cindy

Betty

VIRGINIA

I wish I could tell you that everything was perfect when the relay was over, but once I arrived, I got super-sick. It was as if my body knew it was in a place with round-the-clock expert care, and it was going to make the most of it! I stopped eating, and I had a very bad belly. (I'll spare you the details— let's just say it really hurt, and the people had lots of cleaning up to do.) I got dehydrated, a urinary tract infection, and an eye infection (which meant eyedrops and eyewashes)! I was a disaster.

After lots of tests, the vet figured out that the problem was with my pancreas. The vet gave me medicine and put me on a special diet. Slowly, I felt better, and I started to play outside with Mino and Terrence. I'd lost a lot of my muscle and I was a little hunchbacked, but I could still do most things, just not as fast as before.

And Cindy came to visit me a few weeks later! When she saw me and Mino and Terrence sleeping against one another in our room, she was so happy for me that she hugged every person who was taking care of us.

DON't WORRY, Be HaPPY!
by Buffy

I actually felt great when I got here. My mouth had healed from my dental surgery. I loved living with Jack and Mino. Right away, I liked their scents—they just smelled like friends. Our room quickly felt like home (though Mino was a little barky). We each had our own bed.

But then I got a kind of cough that lots of shelter dogs get, and it took me awhile to get better. At playtime I had to be kept away from other dogs so they didn't get sick, too, but luckily I was already living with Jack and Mino, so we got to stay together. We had a few private outdoor play sessions every day.

But just when my cough finally got better, the people found two lumps under my skin. They were mast cell tumors, which are a kind of cancer. The people got pretty worried about it because most cell cancer can spread

very fast. The vet removed them, and even
though my pretty fur was all shaved and I had
about twenty stitches for two whole weeks, I
remained a very good sport and was still as
graceful as a ballerina.

CHAPTER 6

CLEVER HELPERS

Of course, getting better is tough for anyone if you don't feel safe and comfortable in the first place. Dogs who are blind or deaf (or both) need special help, and the people here have figured out so many cool tricks! And of course I, Mino, have benefited from many of them.

Just like you, dogs have five senses. When we become blind or deaf, we can smell, touch, and taste even better than before.

If our adopters don't know how to help, the people give them information sheets so that dogs like me, Jack, and Buffy can do as well as possible in our new homes.

Jangle catches as well as he always has … as long as the ball smells like beef!

A blind dog's eyes might look like cloudy marbles! Gus has cataracts, probably from diabetes.

Top Five Ways to Help Your Blind and/or Deaf Dog

Blind and deaf dogs can be more independent than you might think. If a dog can smell, taste, and feel, he or she can still play!

Touch

✤ Put long, nonslip carpets (or a path of yoga mats!) on hard floors, connecting all the places your dog goes, so she can feel her way around.

✤ Place plastic mats under food and water bowls so your blind dog knows where to stand.

✤ Small carpet squares in the doorway of each room will make it easier for a blind dog to find the openings.

✤ If possible, line the edge of your yard with mulch, bark chips, or rocks, so it's clear where the yard ends.

Smell

✤ The nose knows! Sniffing lets dogs know what and where things are. Rub scented liquids or oils such as vanilla, citrus, or pine on important areas like doggie doors and the tops and bottoms of staircases.

✤ When going somewhere new, bring along clothes and blankets so your dog can get "grounded" by familiar smells.

✤ Rubbing toys with a favorite food helps your dog "find the fun." You can also buy scented tennis balls!

Sound (if your dog can still hear)

✤ "Jingle bells, jingle bells, jingle all the way!" Make a "blind-dog bracelet" by attaching a jingle bell to a string or a

rubber band (or put one on another dog's collar, so your dog can tell where her friends are). You can also buy tennis balls with jingle bells inside.

❖ As your dog enjoys his favorite activities, use words that help him learn their names (*squirrel, ball, treat, dinner,* and so on).

❖ Put wind chimes at outdoor entrances so your dog knows where home is.

❖ Play with balls that make a sound when they land, and bounce the ball close enough for your dog to follow the sound.

Taste

❖ Until the very end, dogs can still enjoy meals and treats—one of their greatest pleasures. Your dog might especially enjoy eating from your hand.

❖ In a new place, bring your dog to his food and water bowls and touch his chin to their edges so he can learn to find the bowls on his own.

Also, help dogs use their memories. Dogs can quickly "map" their world.

❖ Predictability, routine, and structure will go a long way in helping your dog!

❖ Don't do too much rearranging at home, especially of your dog's bed, food, and water.

❖ In a new place, make sure dogs know their "home bases," such as their bed or crate and their food and water. If they get confused, they always know where the important things are.

When arthritis or joint disease makes sitting, standing, climbing, or walking painful, our people have some great tricks.

When arthritis made sitting, standing, climbing, and walking painful, Kaytee Bell's adoptive family found three good ways to help her get out there and enjoy herself.

Moving Around

Here's how to help your dog enjoy life even when he can't move around comfortably and independently.

- **Create a safe home.** Make your house as easy for your dog as possible. Put in ramps, doggie stairs (so she can still get on beds or couches), nonslip rugs or yoga mats over hard floors, and night-lights near the tops or bottoms of staircases or other tricky places. You can put step stools or specially made "doggie stairs" so your dog can still get onto your bed.

- **Dress up.** Try special nonslip doggie socks or booties to help your furry friend keep his footing. He can also use diapers or "bellybands" for accidents (when you're not around to help him outside).

- **Help her up.** Use slings and hoists to help your dog up and down stairs so she can still go outside.

- **Watch their weight.** Heavier dogs are likely to have more trouble with their joints, and older dogs move less, so they need fewer calories.

- **Try water therapy.** If you have access to a pool, supervised swimming is easy on the joints (for humans, too). It's very relaxing for many dogs, especially ones who once loved swimming. There are even life-vests for dogs who need extra help staying afloat!

Even when our health is complicated, the vet reminds the people that our medical problems usually don't take away our ability to give and receive love.

Tripp the tripod doesn't need any extra help at all! Tripod means "three legs"—and most tripods do just fine.

With twenty-three of us here, someone's always going to the vet. In emergencies, the vet might come to us.

REHABILITATION

Getting HAPPIER

CHAPTER 7

THE SUNSHINE BOYS

I thought I knew everything about humans already . . . the best and the worst. But I've learned so much more here. The people here know exactly how to help you get from "doing really badly" to "doing really well" (and usually pretty fast). That's called rehabilitation (or rehab), and once we're healthy enough (or healthy-ish, ha-ha), the process can really start.

Blossom really blossomed here.

sad abused cold scared

sick depressed

homeless

ONCE, WE WERE

heartbroken injured neglected

forgotten

healthy energetic joyous playful

warm happy healed

dignified protected

trusting

HERE, WE BECOME

confident healed cared for safe relaxed

loved comforted

 Senior Dog Sanctuary of Maryland

Zeus is off to his forever home! When we met Zeus, he was starving, and yet all he wanted to do every day was give out a million kisses. Now Zeus has doubled his weight—and he wants to give two million kisses! Here's what Val says about him: "In this job, you can't think too much about each dog's past. You have to be here with them right now, giving them respect for surviving. Zeus has our respect." #lovewins #heartscanheal #samedog #madeadifferenceforthisone

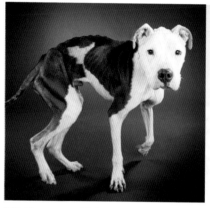 

204 Likes   76 Loves

👍 **Like**   ❤️ **Love**   💬 **Comment**

 Donna M.: What a difference love can make! 🖤🐶🖤🐶

 Tom M.: Thank you, SDSM! 🐾🐾

 Kay M.: My heart's dancing. 😍🐶💜

 Megan T.: The camera doesn't lie! 🦴🦴🦴

Jack and I are the "Sunshine Boys"!

Rehab is about getting to be a normal dog and hang out with other dogs, and to be with good people who know what we need.

If we've spent too much time in shelters, we really appreciate our walks, when we can just sniff anything and everything. Our noses work at least ten thousand times better than people's noses. We know all about the beavers in the dam nearby, even though we can't see them. In my head is a detailed map of all the scents in and around this place, including every person and every dog.

Our backyard is a huge playground. The "grass" looks like the surface of a mini-golf course, but it's made especially for dogs. Pee goes right down into the soil underneath, and poop doesn't get all mushed in. When the people hose it down, it doesn't get muddy or puddly. During the day, you can choose either shade or sun (you can guess my

A big part of rehab is just going on walks.

When they play
in the leaves,
Hip and Hop
feel like jumpy
puppies again.

choice!), and at night it's lit up brightly, like a
football stadium, so we can still play.

And sniffing, snuggling, and sunshine aren't
the only great joys of life here. On summer
days, when the sun is really strong, the
people put on sprinklers and set up kiddie

Sometimes we
get to bring sticks
into the pool!

Whenever Rosie finds a new friend, she invites him or her to play with a "play bow."

pools for us to play in. Outside, we get treats like doggie ice cream and chunks of frozen cantaloupe (perfect for us toothless dogs).

And the people do this other magic thing. They freeze a bunch of our toys in bowls of water, then they put the dome-shaped lump of ice outside. We lick away, and as the ice melts, our toys slowly become free!

Last summer was my rehab. The truth is, it was the best summer of my life. I'd been so sad when my family left me here, and I'd been living with my terrible eyes for such a long time. But last summer I finally felt healthy, and all the fun and love helped me feel sure that I had found my new family.

Samson and Carter are big fans of the buddy system.

CHAPTER 8

THREE-RiNg CIRCUS

Welcome to our own three-ring circus,
starring the three tiny amigos! We've never
let being blind or deaf stop us from having
fun together.

The Three Stooges!

People love to donate toys. They know that being old doesn't mean we want to stop playing. Play keeps our bodies and minds active. We just play a little differently— like, I don't really play rough anymore (it's not as much fun when you have no teeth). Gentle is the name of the game now. But I still enjoy the thrill of the chase. When one smart person rubbed bacon smell on a ball, I showed her what an awesome fetcher I can be!

We get lots of special toys. See, most squeaker toys squeak only when they're bitten, which you need teeth to do. (They're not much fun if you're deaf, either, now are they?) And, of course, most balls are impossible to fetch if you're blind. So each of us has our favorite kind of toy.

FIVE FAVE TOYS

by the Blind, Deaf, and Toothless Pups of SDSM!

1. **Noisy Toys:** There are balls that roll around by themselves and make funny noises. There are toys that talk and make animal sounds on their own, without us pawing them first. There are toys that sound like a baby's rattle or like jingle bells when we shake them. And there are toys that have a squeak that only dogs can hear!

2. **Soft and Floppy Toys:** There's this octopus toy here with long arms, and every time you shake it, you are surprised by all the arms flopping against your face!

3. **Treat-y Toys:** Some balls have small, soft treats inside. We get the treats out

Tawny loves her squeaky donut toy.

Miss Piggy loves her "oinker."

by pushing them with our noses. You really have to concentrate ... but then you get a yummy reward!

4. Squeaker Mats: These have so many squeakers inside them, and we are surprised when we step on them! Then we really get in the mood to play. We use our noses and paws to make the sounds keep going.

5. Squishy, Chewy Toys: Some rubber toys have these little nubs that feel like a nice little massage on your gums—where your teeth once were.

A frozen tennis ball feels great on Pappy's gums.

Speaking of toys, it's almost little dog playtime for the three of us. Hopefully we'll get an hour. We'll continue when we get back!

CHAPTER 9

TRUST AND TOUCH

Lots of us haven't been treated gently in the past, but the people here have some of the best hands ever. They're like professional patters, petters, rubbers, and scritchy-scratchers. And of course they're experts at loving us—they get tons of practice. Almost always there's a volunteer who spends his or her entire shift "loving us up." Sometimes that volunteer is a senior, just like us!

Buffy's complaining that I "always" make her go last because she's the smallest. It's not true. I'm just trying to help out my buddy Jack, because the old fella's slowed down. Also because, honestly, Buffy can get a little bossy. I'm going to stand my ground.

SPARKLES AND TWINKLES
by Buffy

The vets got me healthy, but it was the love and friendship from the people here and the other dogs that got me rehabbed and brought back my old sparkle—and then some! I had two besties, of course—Mino and Jack—but I also made friends with Mazie, the scabby-headed girl who was so scared when she came here that Val had to spend the night in her room. One volunteer, Jenna, really adores me. I love to explore at playtime, but I always run quick-quick-quick to Jenna and let her "love on me." I'm very protective of her. I get that way about whoever's holding me, to be honest—but especially Jenna, because she is PAWSOME!

Jenna was once a cheerleader for a football team . . . now she just cheers me on!

I'm so teeny and flexible (just like a prima ballerina!) that I can get under the gate between the big and little yards, so I can come and go as I please. Which means that I can find Jenna wherever she is. She's always so happy to see me, and she tells me how cute it is that my tongue hangs out. She makes me feel like everything was totally boring until her bestest buddy Buffy finally arrived! The people say that Jenna brought out a new twinkle in my eye.

Well, twinkle, twinkle . . . I *am* a shiny little star!

I do relax sometimes, especially during Book Buddies. One girl always comes up to our room hugging a book to her chest. It's whatever book she's practiced reading at home and in school . . . just for us. Whatever book it is, it's always my favorite of the session. It's just very flattering that she works so hard to prepare for us.

ONCE UPON a TIME
by Jack

Kids help us too, as Book Buddies—they sit with us and read out loud! It's very relaxing, and it especially helps the shy dogs become more sociable and adoptable. And the kids who don't like reading aloud in school can practice with us. We're a great audience—we don't notice mistakes.

We can feel the vibrations of the others' barking when the kids come in, and we're happy to join the pack and add to the noise. But as soon as the kids sit down on their mats in front of our rooms, we quiet down, come right up to the front of our rooms, and settle in for our stories.

Obviously, I can't hear the kids read, but I love Book Buddy time. I like to sniff the kids, and I can tell that Buffy and Mino get totally relaxed, too. I feel our whole room getting quiet and peaceful, as if fat snowflakes have just started falling down in here.

I love putting my head down as the kids read to me, as if it's a bedtime story. The kids don't care if I start to doze off sometimes; they're just happy that we seem to relax and appreciate them.

Afterward, we all play outside with the kids, and I give kisses to everyone—extra for the kids who read to me that day.

The twin volunteers, Colleen and Cassidy, reading two different books to us at the same time! I especially love Snoopy books, *Puppy Place*, *Black Beauty* (told by a horse!), and *Curious George*.

So, as you can tell, Jack, Buffy, and I each got our rehab in different ways. But rehab gets us all ready for the same next step—release, or in our case, adoption. That's when we might go back into the world, a world we might remember as not being so easy for us. But with release, this time we go straight into a loving home of our very own.

PART 4

RELEASE

Getting HOME

CHAPTER 10

3, 2, 1, BLaST OFF!

Since I got here, I've often felt that it would be just fine if I never went to a "real" home. I feel like this *is* home. But I admit it would be nice to sleep in a big bed with people, to roam freely and explore a house, to not always hear so much loud barking around me. And in a home, I might get even more walks and outdoor playtime—maybe even whenever I wanted!

And we really should leave, to make room for new dogs that need help. We know there are too many out there. So eventually, lots of us go into one of the "Three F's"—foster care, fospice care, or a forever home. And they're all good places.

THE THREE F'S

1. **Foster:** A foster home is a temporary situation, until the people at the sanctuary can find us a permanent home. But sometimes our foster mom or dad decides to adopt us for good. That's called a "failed foster," and to the people here, it's the best kind of failure there is!

2. **Fospice:** Hospice is the care you get at the end of your life. You're kept comfortable and pain-free when you're really sick— when the veterinarian knows for sure you won't get better. "Fospice" is foster hospice—a person takes us home so we can have a big bed, lots of love, and people taking good care of us all day and night.

3. **Forever Home:** The name says it all! It's an "official" adoption—the people keep us for the rest of our lives.

SENIORS FOR SENIORS

This is a special kind of fostering program. If a senior citizen wants to have a dog, the staff helps make a good match—a calm dog that's healthy enough and doesn't need much activity. If it gets too hard for the person to take care of that dog, or if the person has to go into the hospital or a retirement or nursing home, the sanctuary just takes the dog back. And if a senior citizen in the area has to leave their dog here because they're moving to retirement home or a nursing home that doesn't allow dogs, Val will take that dog in and bring him or her to visit the person!

No matter which of the F's happen to us (and to tell you the truth, "foster" and "forever home" kinda feel the same to us), we keep our SDSM collar on. Once a sanctuary dog, always a sanctuary dog—we're always welcome back here, no matter what. Once we've come through the doors of this place, we have a home for the rest of our lives.

But I, Mino the Pom Bomb, am going to get the best of both worlds. I get to have a home and come back to visit all the time.

I'm the luckiest dog ever, because Val has decided to foster me.

My lungs haven't been working well lately, so he wants to watch me closely. But I don't let my lungs ruin my fun. Even when I have to lie down for longer than I'd like, I get excited thinking about how, when I'm home with Val and his wife, Margee, I'm also going to be with Sunni, Chip, and Chance again—all sanctuary dogs! Margee's visited me here, too, and she likes me already.

Val's the best friend I've ever had. I think he should be made King of the World. Actually, that might not work, because I'd actually like that job. I'll figure something out later; I always do.

Oh, what a surprise—Buffy's bugging me. She's announcing over and over that she must tell her release story. And I agree, she really should, 'cause it's an excellent one.

QUEEN JENNA
by Princess Buffy

OMG, can you guess? Three cheers for my darling Jenna, Jenna, Jenna. Since we met, she's known that those cancer lumps could come back any minute, and they could start taking over. She says she wants me to have a home for as long as I live, whether it's a week or a year (maybe more)! She's wanted to foster me for a while now, but she's been fostering a dog who had his leg removed. Now she's finally found that tripod a forever home, so there's room for me! Go Mr. Tripod! Go Jenna! Go me!

And … because good things happen in threes …

BLaNKeTS FOREVER

by Jack

A few days ago, a lady named Dana and her husband and teenage sons read about me online and came to see me. Dana came into our room, sat down on the floor, wrapped me in a new blanket she'd brought, and held me for a long time. She even took me outside for fresh air, and I got to stay in her arms, in my blanket. She felt and smelled like the perfect human.

Right then and there, she let me know that she wanted me to join her family. And she let me know that all their dogs and cats (all seniors!) sleep in their beds with them—I'll have three beds and a few couches to choose from. And … I'll have all the pillows and blankets I want.

The people think I'm developing "old dog syndrome," so they gave Dana this information sheet. Dana's had plenty of seniors, and she assured them that she'll meet any challenges that come our way. All that matters is that I'm happy and comfortable, she said. I didn't hear her say these things, but I felt her arms tell me loud and clear.

Helping Dogs with "Old Dog Syndrome"

After age eleven, more than half of all dogs develop symptoms that are similar to Alzheimer's disease in humans. Their personalities may suddenly change. They may get confused, scared, or anxious. They might pace, walk in circles, hide, shake, or tremble. They might get lost in once-familiar spaces, lose their appetite, have more accidents inside, forget simple commands like "sit" or "stay," or sleep more during the day (and bark all night!). It can be hard for everyone, but there are ways to help:

1. **Talk with your vet.** There are medicines that can help.

2. **Stay with a routine.** Senior dogs do best when their lives are predictable.

3. **Exercise their bodies.** Even a slow five-minute walk every day helps. If possible, playing with other dogs does, too.

4. **Challenge their brains.** Provide toys that keep their minds active, switching the toys every so often so there's something new. Try food puzzles—containers that hold food or treats.

5. **Show love, patience, and understanding.** Your affection and presence make a world of difference to your dog.

Anyway, it's finally our turn for release. I'm so happy we're all leaving at the same time and that we'll still get to visit sometimes. I would just hate to leave my pals behind.

Snapple with a volunteer, Joseph, at his first adoption fair. He was adopted soon after!

Our adoption party! Sometimes the dog who gets adopted gets a cake from a dog bakery, and every dog gets a piece!

CHAPTER 11

SUNSET STORIES

Of course, all the F's come to an end sooner or later (hopefully later!). You see, "release" can also mean letting go—eventually our bodies just let go of life. I've heard the people say that the day their dog dies is one of the saddest days of their whole lives.

We just learned that Terrence died.

At the sanctuary entrance near the beaver dam is the Rainbow Garden, a rock garden where we will be buried. Each dog buried there gets his or her name engraved on a river rock. I never pee on any of those rocks.

Val put our Rainbow Garden close to the sanctuary entrance. He says there shouldn't be any secret about how our stories end.

He feels good that even if our lives have been sad, we've all spent our last months or weeks or days at the sanctuary (or in a good home), feeling loved and cared for.

Even if we've already been adopted, our new families sometimes want to bury us here, with our old friends, in this place that was so important to us. The people believe different things about what happens when we die. Lots of people here believe in the Rainbow Bridge.

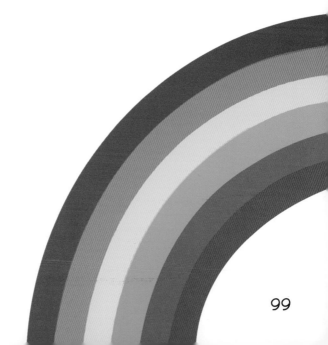

The Rainbow Bridge

Before they go to heaven, animals go to a place called the Rainbow Bridge, which is just this side of heaven.

There are meadows and hills. They run and play with other dogs. There are lots of food, water, and sunshine, and they're warm and comfortable. They are healthy, whole, and strong again, just as we remember them in our dreams of days and times gone by. They're happy and content, although they each miss a special person (or people) they had to leave behind.

They're busy playing and enjoying themselves, but every so often one dog suddenly stops playing and looks into the distance. His bright eyes are intent, and his eager body quivers. He begins to run from the group, flying over the green grass, faster and faster. He has spotted his person.

When the two reunite, they hug and hug, never to be parted again. His happy kisses cover his person's face; his person's hands caress the animal's beloved head, and they look into each other's eyes. They were apart for so long, but they were never absent from each other's hearts.

Then they cross the Rainbow Bridge together.
—Author unknown

 Senior Dog Sanctuary of Maryland

We are heartbroken to announce that Terrence has peacefully crossed the Rainbow Bridge. He died in his wonderful foster home, surrounded by love.

Terrence came to us as a stray and somehow always managed to be underfoot even though his back had been badly hurt. When he was outside, he wanted to come back in. When he was in his room, he barked to go out!

Terrence had good days and bad days. On his good days, he would run and trot. On his bad days, you knew he had played too hard the day before. But in his last days, Terrence wasn't alone for one minute.

That's how the end of life is here at the sanctuary, too. Sometimes we'll sleep in dogs' rooms with them. If volunteers and staff members are not working that day, they will come by to kiss the dogs goodbye and love them up all day. We hold them as they slip away, so in their very last moments they know they are loved and respected for who they are . . . just because they are dogs. #pawprintsonourhearts #terrence

203 Likes   76 Loves

👍 **Like**   ❤️ **Love**   💬 **Comment**

Eve E.: RIP, sweet guy. 🖤🖤

Debbie G.: We'll miss you so much, Terrence. 🐾🐾

Bill B.: We all loved you a lot, Terrence. 🖤🖤🖤

Roger W.: Wait for us at the Rainbow Bridge, Terrence! 🦴🦴🦴

When a dog dies at home, sometimes their family will bring their favorite treats to all the dogs here. I like the treats, of course, but I hate it when my friends die. I don't get why it has to happen. The people say it just does...just because.

Buffy and Jack and I may be small dogs, but we've lived big lives. We've had good times and bad, but through it all, we've used our spirits to love big. In the end, we got all that big love right back.

And hey! It's not over yet for us. We've still got more life in us, and we intend to make the most of whatever time we've got left.

CHAPTER 12

READY, SET, LOVE!

So, new resident (or residents) of this room, you've just begun your adventure. No matter how you feel right now, remember everything we said about what happens here. Look at the way all these stories ended.

Okay, we've gotta go now, but we're going to have a little reunion party here soon, and we'll come see you! You don't need us to say good luck; you're in the lucky room already. But good luck anyway! (And speaking just for myself, I hope you make friends who are as good company for you as Jack and Buffy have been for me. If you do, you'll be a very lucky dog.)

You've got lots of people (and us Three Blind Mice) rooting for you!

REUNION
by Mino

Hello again!

As I mentioned, Jenna, Val, and Dana understood how terrific our little trio was, so today they brought us back together for a little reunion party right here at the sanctuary. We all smelled one another right away, and it felt just like the old days. It was home, but in a different way from our new homes.

We walked outside together and put our noses right to the ground. I smelled the beavers again! And the people were so happy to see us. We got lots of kisses, hugs, and treats, and everyone took photos. We felt like Hollywood stars on the red carpet!

Big surprise—Jack slept in Dana's arms, wrapped in his favorite blanket, through most of the party. But it was okay. We knew he was there. We spent most of the sunny day outside and visited with some of our friends on their walks. But then we went to see our old room, and—how about that—look who else is here! That's right . . . you guys! Hello, Bella and Keno. I see the people put

you in with Mazie! She's a great lady and a good friend of Buffy's. Oh look, she and Buffy get to play outside together now.

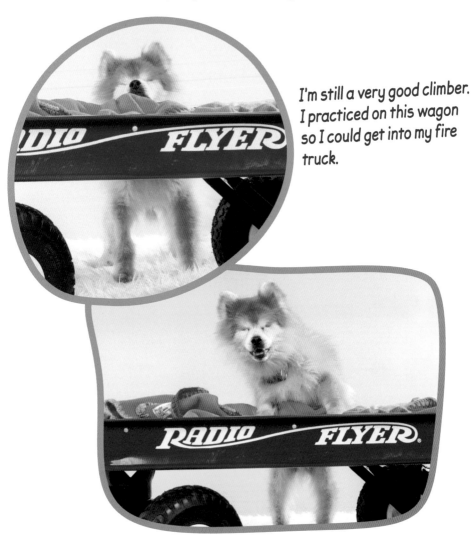

I'm still a very good climber. I practiced on this wagon so I could get into my fire truck.

Life's a wild ride, isn't it? Enjoy, guys!

Anyway, I never did figure out why some humans don't treat us well, or why we can't live forever. But I've stopped trying to understand. I'm going to spend the rest of my energy on giving and getting love from all my good people. For me, it's always been about the love, anyway.

WHERE WE ARE NOW

Senior Dog Sanctuary of Maryland

Mazie just got adopted by Susan, who is our volunteer Jenna's mom. Jenna adopted Buffy a few months ago, and now Susan drops Mazie off at Jenna's every day before work for "daycare"—which, for Buffy and Mazie, just means playing all day long the way they used to.

---

204 Likes   76 Loves

👍 Like   ❤️ Love   💬 Comment

Judy J.: Yay for Mazie, Keno, and Bella! 🖤 🐶 🖤 🐶

Brian M.: So happy these guys found their "furever" homes! 🐾

Nancy M.: Seems like a very lucky room indeed! 😍 🐶 🖤

Patrick W.: Congratulations to the pups and their new people! 🦴

JACK

Dana knew exactly how to make me feel right at home. She's always making my special treats, and I've gained a pound! She stomps around the house so I can feel the vibrations, and when she's near, she lets me smell her so I know it's

her. I still get my exercise outside, but my balance is a little worse. So I just shuffle between Dana's legs!

The teenagers call me Captain Jack. They think I act like I'm the captain of this ship. (I know it's a house, but sometimes I get

confused.) If I want to be picked up, I just bark until someone picks me up. They say I walk like a drunken sailor, because I stumble and wobble. (But look—I'm fifteen and I can still walk!) They giggle at my funny low growl, and they call me Grumble Guy when I grumble at the refrigerator. Dana calls it "arguing with the fridge." Another dog here just sits by the heater all day, which I call "guarding the radiator." Hey, we all have our jobs.

One of my favorite things in my new home is feeling the vibrations of the door opening and closing, because that tells me my people are home. Usually, the first thing they do is come over to my little bed, pet me, kiss me, and tell me what a good boy I am. Then I go right back to sleep.

I've been having very sweet dreams since I got here.

BUFFY

Well, obviously, Jenna is the sun and moon. Or pure sunshine. Or the star I once wished upon that one time when I was alone and scared. Or all those things! I feel like my home is my castle.

I have a new
buddy here!

Since Jenna took me home, I've become a Velcro dog. I follow her everywhere, including the bathroom. If someone else is holding me and Jenna is nearby, I'm polite, but I spend the whole time just trying to figure out a way back to her. I'd choose being held by Jenna over my many toys any day. I use the doggie door to go out to pee and poop, but I rush right back inside as fast as I can, to be where I belong. When Jenna showers, I sit nicely on the bathmat, waiting for her to come out. Jenna's like my own personal goddess, and she tells everyone that she loves me just as much as I love her!

Jenna has two big dogs, too, George and Skylar. They're huge! They make me miss my little blind mice friends. If they make me mad, I'll stand up to them, but I've had to accept that in many ways George is the boss around here. Sometimes he licks my fur, and

I just have to tolerate it. But when we all go for long walks, I'm always the one in the lead, and I'm the boss lady—I protect them from any strangers approaching my pack, LOL. And sometimes I cuddle with them. Best of all, I play with Mazie every day.

I gained a pound, too. Now I weigh eight pounds, and I have a little potbelly!

My favorite spot is the Pillow and Blanket Mountain on the couch. I made up a hide-and-seek game—I burrow into the pile of blankets and pillows so Jenna can't see me. She calls

I love to hide on Jenna's couch!

me, and I jump out from behind a pillow or under a blanket! Then she picks me up and I nuzzle my head under her chin to make sure she feels my love. Besides being with Jenna, the other thing I like to do is lie on my back and show everyone my tummy. I wiggle around and rub my back against the carpet.

A few weeks after I got to Jenna's, she found another one of my cancer lumps, and I had to go back to the vet and have it removed. The humans were really freaked out, but it wasn't a big deal, at least for me. Now they seem to have stopped worrying. Maybe just by being myself, I taught them to enjoy the good times we're having together. It's just my way of being me!

MiNO

Well, here I finally am at the Rainbow Bridge.
I'm waiting patiently for my favorite people.
I was actually feeling like my skippy self
until the day I died. But then my little body
just started to quit on me. Suddenly, the
insulin shots wouldn't keep my sugar level
down. The people couldn't control my blood
pressure, and my kidneys and lungs weren't
working well enough either.

As Val and the others waited for the vet to
arrive, they tried to listen closely to what I
might be trying to tell them. There had been
plenty of times when it seemed like the end
for me, and they said to each other, "We
won't tell Mino it's over unless he tells us it's
over. He still has too much spirit left in him!"

And they had been right every time. I never
wanted to stop being alive! I wanted more
love, more treats, more belly rubs, more sun

on my face, more kids reading to me, more things to sniff, more snuggles with Jack, more of everything!

And I'd been having such a good time living at Val and Margee's. Margee laughed at the sound my nails made on their hard floors: *Tap, tap, tap! Click, click, click!* Big Chance looked after me in the yard. I still loved to explore, but there were some prickly briars and holly bushes, and when I got too close, Chance nudged me away. I liked to stand on top of the big mulch mound, point my nose to the sun. I felt like king of the mountain.

In the end, Val wound up adopting me.

But one day things changed. All of a sudden, I just didn't care about being king of the mountain anymore. I didn't want more of anything. For the first time, I felt ready to say

goodbye, and the people and the vet knew it for sure. Everyone cried, but they were glad that they could help me die peacefully. Val held me as the others sang to me, and then the vet gave me a shot. It didn't hurt. And everything I'd heard about the Rainbow Bridge turned out to be true.

So that's the whole story, beginning to end, of me—Mino the Great. I did a great job just being a dog. Online and in person, I taught thousands of humans that senior dogs make great new family members. I left my pawprints all over people's hearts. And they sure did leave their handprints on mine!

My body may be in the Rainbow Garden, but now my heart is everywhere.

Friends forever!

A LETTER FROM THE AUTHOR
BECOMING REAL

I'm the type who stops to say hello to every dog on the street, even if I'm in a hurry. "Can I pet your dog?" I ask the owners. "What's her name? Where did you find her?" I love it that people and dogs can become friends so quickly. When I started writing this book, I began to notice and ask about the dogs' ages, and if they were seniors, I asked even more questions.

I haven't had a dog since I was young, when my mom and stepfather rescued Samoyeds (I have cats at home now). Samoyeds are big, smiling dogs, as fluffy and as white as snow. There were always two at a time (when one died, my mom and stepfather would adopt another), and everyone around town knew them—they were hard to miss. Kids and adults approached with questions, and my mom always explained the idea of breed rescue. On snowy days, people commented that the dogs must be happy and asked if they pulled sleds. People pointed out that they looked like polar bears. Most of my mom and stepfather's

Samoyeds lived a long time (although, because their muzzles were already white, you couldn't see their "sugarfaces"!).

When I was a kid, my mom would read me *The Velveteen Rabbit* by Margery Williams Bianco. She always got teary when we got to the page where the Skin Horse (a worn-out old stuffed animal in a boy's room) explains to the Velveteen Rabbit (a newer stuffed animal) about how, when one is loved well for a very long time, one becomes "real." Now I realize that she was getting emotional about all her senior dogs. Here's what the Skin Horse said:

"Generally, by the time you are Real, most of your hair has been loved off, and your eyes drop out and you get loose in the joints and very shabby. But these things don't matter at all, because once you are Real you can't be ugly, except to people who don't understand."

As an adult, I've known and loved many "real" senior dogs, like Mo, Lottie, Chloe, Cookie, Kaytee Bell,

Kojak, Cassie, Elvis, Charlie, Ruby, Bandie, and Buddy. I met many more when I started visiting the Senior Dog Sanctuary of Maryland. On my first visit, Val met me at the train station, holding balloons so I could find him easily. Now I think of those balloons as the beginning of a celebration of the dogs'—and the staff's—"realness."

Once, at the sanctuary, I met Mino, Jack, and Buffy in their little room. I remembered the conversation between the Skin Horse and the Velveteen Rabbit, and I knew right away that their spirits were big enough to narrate this book. I just hope I've told their stories as well as the old Skin Horse told his.

— Kama Einhorn

My mom, Karen, with Kimo the senior Samoyed

A COUPLE OF QUICK QUESTIONS FOR VAL LYNCH

Q: Why senior dogs and not all dogs?

A: *Well, I'm not exactly up for taking care of puppies! Now that I'm older, I see the seniors as a reflection of myself. I'm slower; I want to sleep and relax more. They tend to be as active as I am. We're on the same wavelength.*

Q: What is something you love about dogs?

A: *Even after humans have betrayed them, they are still ready to love us again. Also, most humans want to give dogs love and affection. We do that, and we add another important piece—respect for where they are in their lives. When you show someone respect, it allows them to be the best they can be.*

HØW YØU CAN HELP

There are other sanctuaries in the United States just for senior dogs (see page 135), but if you don't live near one, you can still help the senior dogs in your local shelters by donating supplies. You can call or go online to find out what they need, but most shelters and sanctuaries usually ask for:

- Towels and blankets
- Water and food bowls
- Laundry detergent
- Toys
- Leashes and collars
- Brushes/grooming tools
- Pet beds
- Blankets, towels
- Garbage bags
- Wet or dry food
- Dog treats
- Cleaning supplies
- Old newspapers

- Paper towels and toilet paper

- Hand sanitizer

- Office supplies

- Gift cards for online pet supply stores

But you can create and assemble your own donations, too. You might deliver them in a bag or basket along with a note to the dogs. This toy and game are perfect for blind, deaf, and toothless dogs:

Crinkle Socks. Slip an empty water bottle into a sock! When the dog puts his or her mouth on it, it makes a crinkle sound that some dogs love. You can rub a scent on the sock for blind dogs.

Muffins for Pups. Help senior dogs keep their brains active! You'll need a muffin tin (for six to twelve muffins), tennis balls (six to twelve), and small treats with a strong scent. (For small dogs, use mini–muffin pans and Ping-Pong balls.) In your donation, include a note explaining the game:

1. Cut the treats into small pieces and put a piece in each hole of the muffin tin.

2. Let the dog eat one treat from the tin. Then teach the dog how to play. Place a tennis ball on

top of the treat and slightly lift a ball so he can sniff the hidden treat (especially important for blind dogs).

3. Then put the tennis ball back on and encourage him to move the tennis ball with his paw or nose to get the treat.

Some dogs will learn the game faster than others. If needed, lift a tennis ball now and then to remind the dog how to play.

Tripp loves his treats.

You can also make and deliver the same treats that Mino and the other diabetic dogs love:

Diabetic Doggie Treats

Courtesy of Jack's guardian, Dana Smith

Ask a grownup to help you. This recipe makes about fifty "cookies."

1. Blend ½ cup whole wheat flour, 2 eggs, and 2 jars of beef baby food (containing only beef, water, and cornstarch in the ingredient list) in a blender.

2. Spread the mixture on a small baking sheet or glass casserole dish (parchment paper will keep it from sticking).

3. Bake 15 minutes at 350° or until the center is firm.

4. Cool and cut into small squares with a pizza cutter (the treats will feel spongy). Store in refrigerator (or freeze them in a plastic container or bag).

Two other big ways to help all dogs:

Remind grownups of the importance of spaying and neutering animals, so there won't be so many homeless dogs in the first place. Lack of space in animal shelters is the main reason why senior dogs have such a tough time.

If your family wants to get a dog, remind them that it's not necessary to buy one. Shelters and sanctuaries are full of great dogs! If you've got your heart set on a certain breed, search "breed rescue" (with the name of the breed) online, and you'll find tons of purebred dogs who need homes.

GLOSSARY

arthritis: a joint condition that can cause aches and pains and make moving difficult

diabetes: a disease in which a mammal has too much sugar in his or her blood

foster: to care for temporarily

glaucoma: an eye disease caused by too much pressure behind the eyes

hospice: a way of caring for a living thing when it's very sick and doctors know for sure that it won't get better

insulin: a chemical that helps sugar get into mammals' cells for energy

muzzle: a dog's snout, its nose/mouth area

protect: to keep from harm

recover: to get better

rehabilitate: to return to one's natural condition

release: to let go

rescue: to save or help

sanctuary: a safe place

treatment: the way a person cares for or behaves toward others

welfare: the health and happiness of a person or animal

GOT A SUGARFACE IN YOUR LiFE?

If your own dog is a senior or if you know any senior dogs, you already know lots of ways to make them happy and comfortable. Try making them these treats. Check with a grownup to make sure the dog's diet allows these things. A grownup might need to ask a vet because many vets recommend very specific diets for senior dogs, and they're all different.

Roo still loves the taste of pork.

Summer Treats for Toothless Dogs

You'll need a blender and something to freeze the mixtures in, such as an ice-cube tray; a muffin pan with cupcake liners; empty, clean Styrofoam egg cartons; small paper cups; or any small plastic container. Ask a grownup to help you blend all the ingredients together. Then scoop or pour the mixture into your containers and freeze.

- **Apple Freeze:** ¾ cup apples, ¼ cup low-sodium peanut butter, 1 cup ice cubes.

- **Peanut Butter Ice:** 2 small containers of plain,

low-fat yogurt, ½ cup of low-sodium organic peanut butter (no additives), 1 small jar of banana baby food (or a small ripe banana), and 1 tablespoon of honey.

- **Cold Chicken Cubes:** 2 cooked, chopped chicken breasts, 2 cups water, 1 tablespoon dried parsley.

- **Fish Delish:** 15-ounce can of tuna (packed in water), 2 cups of plain nonfat yogurt, 1 tablespoon dried parsley.

- **Summery Meals:** Mix ¼ cup canned dog food with ⅓ cup beef or chicken broth.

Hip and Hop work up an appetite.

You don't even need a blender for these:

- **Broth Cubes**: Freeze ½ cup low-sodium beef or chicken broth and ½ cup water. You can add cooked, finely chopped broccoli, green beans, or carrots, or finely chopped tuna, chicken, or beef—it sinks to the bottom and makes a nice surprise once the broth is licked away!

- **Icy Surprise**: Dice up banana, carrot, apple, or blueberries. Fill the ice-cube tray halfway with water, add the fruits and/or veggies, and freeze.

- **Kibble Pops**: Soak regular dry food in just enough water (or low-sodium broth) to cover about half the kibble. Let the kibble absorb almost all of the water, then freeze.

Justin and Gabrielle wait patiently for their treats.

And toothless dogs like these cookies all
year long!

No-Chew Peanut Butter "Brownies"

1½ cups water

½ cup vegetable oil

2 eggs

3–5 tablespoons peanut butter (up to you)

2 teaspoons vanilla

2 cups flour (oat flour, if pup has wheat allergies)

1 cup oat flour or oatmeal

Mashed banana (optional)

Blend wet ingredients (including banana, if you're
using it). Stir dry ingredients into the wet mixture.
Pour into ungreased glass pan and bake 20 minutes
at 400°. Let cook, cut with pizza roller, put in
baggies, and refrigerate.

LEARN MORE

The Senior Dog Sanctuary of Maryland is a temporary or permanent home for homeless dogs. The dogs' guardians (owners) may have died or gotten sick, and no one else was able to take them. They may have been abandoned or abused. Senior dogs don't do very well in regular shelters, and they are much less likely to be adopted than younger dogs are. Many people would rather adopt puppies, and the senior dogs get overlooked.

Val Lynch, the founder, is a senior citizen himself. He, his wife, Margee, and their three kids have always had dogs in their family. When Val retired from his lifetime of service in the US Air Force, he and his son Greg decided to take rescue to another level. That's when they started SDSM, which looks like a regular house with a big backyard. But it's no regular house!

The Senior Dog Sanctuary of Maryland has frequent tours. Visit the sanctuary's website: seniordogsanctuary.com. Also check out its Facebook page.

Besides SDSM, there are other senior dog sanctuaries (though some are foster networks and don't have actual buildings). All have lots of photos on social media!

- Shep's Place Senior Dog Sanctuary: *shepsplace.org*.

- Susie's Senior Dogs: *susiesseniordogs.com*.

- Old Friends Senior Dog Sanctuary: *ofsds.org*.

- Sugar Faces Senior Dog Rescue: *sugarfacesrescue.org*.

- The Sanctuary for Senior Dogs: *sanctuaryforseniordogs.org*.

- Heath's Haven Rescue: *heathshavenrescue.com*.

- The Senior Dogs Project: *srdogs.com*.

- House with a Heart Senior Pet Sanctuary: *housewithaheart.com*.

- Marty's Place Senior Dog Sanctuary: *martysplace.org*.

- The Grey Muzzle Organization: *greymuzzle.org*.

"Senior dogs are survivors. Many dogs here have lived through horrible, stressful situations, but they don't come away bitter or angry. They still want our affection, and it's an honor to give it to them.

"Dogs have evolved to be 'man's best friend.' Most have 'served' humans their whole lives, loving them no matter what. In their last years, these dogs deserve their dignity. They deserve our respect."

—Val Lynch, SDSM founder

BiBLI⊖GRAPHY

Anderson, Eileen. *Remember Me? Loving and Caring for a Dog with Canine Cognitive Dysfunction.* Little Rock, Ark.: Bright Friends Productions, 2015.

Coffey, Laura T. *My Old Dog: Rescued Pets with Remarkable Second Acts.* Novato, Calif.: New World Library, 2015.

Klonsky, Jane Sobel. *Unconditional: Older Dogs, Deeper Love.* Washington, DC: National Geographic, 2016.

Morgan, Diane. *The Living Well Guide for Senior Dogs: Everything You Need to Know for a Happy & Healthy Companion.* Neptune City, N.J.: TFH Publications, 2007.

Shojai, Amy. *Complete Care for Your Aging Dog.* Furry Muse Publishing, 2003.

Stanton, Erin. *Susie's Senior Dogs.* New York: Gallery Books, 2016.

Thorne, Pete. *Old Faithful: Dogs of a Certain Age.* New York: Harper, 2015.

PHOTO CREDITS

All photographs by Virgil Ocampo except for:

dedication page, 7, 75, 68 (bottom), 87, 131:
Greg Lynch

17: Shutterstock

25: courtesy of Val Lynch

35: courtesy of Senior Dog Sanctuary of Maryland

39 (top): Humane Society of Pulaski County

45: Sid Keiser

46, 47: Shutterstock

58: Shutterstock

66: Avi Drabkin

83: Eve Emerson

111, 113: Jenna Patcella

115 (bottom left): Shutterstock

123: Kama Einhorn

ACKNOWLEDGMENTS

Special thanks to:

Doug Baer

Karen Ball

Jennifer Stehr Basiliko

Pam Bresnahan

Dave Crawford

Cindy Eller

Eve Emerson

Cassidy Gill

Colleen Gill

Ashley Hangliter

Debbie Jones

Kevin Mattero

Dennis Moses, LVT

Jenna Patcella

Mary Rawlings, DVM

Senator Ed Reilly

Nancy Ruth, DVM

Noelle Salmon

Christine Sandberg

Shelter Animals Count

Jessica Shraibman

Amey Silkworth

Dana Smith

Lisa Staruszkiewicz

Stay Pet Resort

Barbara Turner

Jim Weaver

Chris Weinstein

Jessica Whitacre

- Jewelry and costumes donated by Artisans and Crafters Supporting Animals in Need

- The groomers of Dog Thrive, Gambrills, Maryland

- Humane Society of Pulaski County, who first rescued Jack and Buffy

INDEX

⟨⟨ TRUE TALES of RESCUE ⟩⟩

Available now!

Coming soon!

Kama Einhorn is a humane
educator, animal welfare
advocate, and author of
more than forty books
for children and teachers.
Animals are her people.
She lives in Brooklyn,
New York.

⤺⋮ TRUE TALES of RESCUE ⋮⤻

Available now!

Coming soon!

RACCOONS REMEMBER

ANTEATER ADVENTURE

Kama Einhorn is a humane educator, animal welfare advocate, and author of more than forty books for children and teachers. Animals are her people. She lives in Brooklyn, New York.